PLENTY OF TIME

PLENTY OF TIME

Brian Morse

Illustrations by Gunvor Edwards

The Bodley Head
London

1 3 5 7 9 10 8 6 4 2

Copyright © text Brian Morse 1994

Copyright © illustrations Gunvor Edwards 1994

Brian Morse and Gunvor Edwards have asserted their rights under the Copyright, Designs and Patents Act, 1988 to be identified as the author and illustrator of this work

First published in the United Kingdom 1994
by The Bodley Head Children's Books
Random House, 20 Vauxhall Bridge Road, London SW1V 2SA

Random House Australia (Pty) Limited
20 Alfred Street, Milsons Point, Sydney,
New South Wales 2061, Australia

Random House New Zealand Limited
18 Poland Road, Glenfield,
Auckland 10, New Zealand

Random House South Africa (Pty) Limited
PO Box 337, Bergvlei 2012, South Africa

Random House UK Limited Reg. No. 954009

A CIP catalogue record for this book is available from
the British Library

ISBN 0 370 31881 1

Printed in Great Britain by Clays Ltd, St Ives plc

Contents

Dawn	9
Good Morning	10
Yawn	11
Carthorses	12
Pigeons	13
First Day	14
Pin Drop	15
Keep Your Feet Dry	16
The Dragon in the Playground	18
Wrong	19
The Crane	20
Earth Eater	22
Supermarket Robert	24
A Lesson	25
Uphill, Downhill	26
Following the Smells	28
The Farm Park	29
Mum's on a Diet	30
Special Request	31
Dad's Bald	32
Short Back and Sides	34
Names	35
Last Day of Term	36
Home Time	38
Thank You	39
Bye, Cat	40
Plenty of Time	42
Saturdays	44
Small Talk	45
History	46
Sledging	48

Windy Day	49
Chocolate Santa	50
What, Me?	51
When I was a Baby	52
Trees	54
Fox	56
Old Man's Song	57
Weekends	58
Beach Howl	59
Out of the Sun	60
Manners	62
Mum Says	63
After the Party	64
Get You	65
Snow	66
In Moonlight	67
I Love it Late at Night	68
Lost in a Forest	70
Candle	71
Sleep	72
Lullaby	74
Kipper	76
Night-Time	77

for Jesse and Joseph
and Sarah and Daniel

Dawn

Mist rolls past
the curtained windows.

At the end of the garden
the fox lifts its head.
It listens to
the dew drip
tick tock, tick tock.
Swift-pawed
it turns towards bed.

I saw it first!
a sparrow shouts from the gutter.
Me! Me! Me!
I saw the sun first!
I was the winner this morning!

Good Morning

Good morning!
I'm the dog in the hall.

I sleep by the wall
and wait all night long

for them to come downwards.
Them sleep up stairs

on silky sheets
and when the light's high

down they come tumbling.
Then it's all feet

and lacing boots
and *get down, boy!*

Feet take them walking
and me on the end

of my leathery thread
chasing smells of brushy tails

and whisker spit-faces.
After all's quiet.

Machine takes them
long rolling day-long walk.

Up stairs then.
Him sleep on silky sheets.

Him dream.

Yawn

Red cave
with a tunnel at the back.

Gappy teeth.

A tongue,
all curled.

Lips
in a big
O.

Morning, sunshine!
Time to get up!

YAWN!

Carthorses

They lie side by side
all night in the field,
heads turned towards the five-barred gate
like dogs waiting for their morning walk.
As Kipper runs round them
they steam
in the early air.

Pigeons

The man with the pigeons
        at the end of the street
feeds them every morning
        at half past eight.

Where he appears from
        I've never seen
but the pigeons know.
        As the church clock strikes

in a wave of rustling feathers
        they flock down to his feet,
a rush of shining eyes,
        and darting beaks.

Then suddenly he's gone,
        his satchel empty.
Cracking their wings, the pigeons rise
        and fan out through the city.

First Day

The street growled.
Traffic snarled
and roared and groaned.
My satchel weighed a ton.
Above my head
a voice complained,
'Darren! Why are you dragging your feet?'

'Because I'm four and a half,
it's my first day at school,
that's why!' I thought.
'Don't you remember anything?'
'Hurry up do,' the voice said.
'And yes, I remember, very well.
But this is a hard day for me too,
losing my little boy.'

Then I remembered
all my friends from nursery,
the whole gang would be there —
Robot Robert, Gary the Giant,
Sega Sam and Desperate Dan.
I pulled on Mum's hand.
'Come on!' I shouted. 'Run!
We're going to be late!'

Pin Drop

It was so noisy before school,
the teacher with the bell shouted,
'Everyone, shut up!
That includes you too, parents!
It's starting to rain.
You don't want everyone to get wet
waiting for silence — *do you?*'

Mum said,
'You could have heard a pin drop!'
What I heard
was the quiet
pattering about the playground
desperately looking for somewhere to hide
from that terrible voice.

Keep Your Feet Dry

'Wear your hat,' Mum said,
'and step over the puddles.
Right over.
No accidentally
landing in the middle!
Keep dry or you'll get a chill.
You don't want a cold
for your holiday.'

Of course I didn't
but Mark from number 55 said,
'Don't be so stupid.
My Mum says getting wet
doesn't give you a chill.
It's an old wives' tale.
And who made you wear that hat?
It's horrible.
You look a right wally!'

That was what I thought,
so I took it off
and walked through
every puddle
I could find
between here and school,
and a few others,
and the ditch
that runs along
the edge
of the playing field.
That was ace.

The water came
right over my ankles.

When Miss Dixon
saw the mess I was in
she shouted
at the top of her voice
and made me dress
in the socks and trousers
from Class 8's
dressing-up box.
I hated that.
Of course Mark
got to school as dry as a bone.

His Mum's wrong.
Getting wet does give you a chill.
Getting wet does give you a cold.

The Dragon in the Playground

How slow can a clock tick?
How slowly can a lesson drag?
I was staring out of the window,
dreaming of a different place,
when, in a flurry of dust,
a dragon landed.
Only me looking
— so no one saw it except me,
me and the caretaker's cat.

At first it hid behind the sports shed,
then it got bolder,
sniffed some crisps
and gobbled a broken biscuit.
Its green scales glittered in the sun,
its spiky tail waved —
just like the cat's.
It was beginning to really enjoy itself.

It crunched two apple cores
and began to investigate the caretaker's dustbin.
A tiny breath of dragon-fire
licked about its lips,
the blue of flame about to kindle.

I shouted,
'Look, Miss! Look!
See what's in the playground! Please!'

'What is it?' teacher said.
'I'm coming!'
But by the time she got to my place
the dragon had flown off.

Wrong

Kevin Cooper tricked me.
He said teacher had gone.
He said, 'Throw it! Go on!'
But she hadn't.
She was just bending down.

'Who threw that?' the teacher shouted.
'That nearly hit me!
What naughty boy did it?
Own up! Own up!'

No one owned up.
We stayed in at play.
We stayed in all day.
But why should I own up?
I'm no boy.

The Crane

Its long neck reaches out high over the houses
and buildings
At   and
the   picks
end   up
of   bricks
the   and
l   boxes.
o   It moves them from
here   to   there.
n
g
day
the
crane
keeper
climbs
down
all
the
steps
of
the
l
o
n
g
ladder
to
the

ground and
        zooms
                    away
                        home
                            to his tea
                                    in
                                        his
                                            car
as fast as he can.

Earth Eater

The digger
puts its
yellow chin
on the ground
and pushes.

With
a clank
its neck
jerks up.
For a moment
it thinks
then
slowly,
as if it was tasting,
eats
a mouthful
of earth.

Ugh! That
tasted horrid!
Its long neck
swings,
looking for
a place
to put it
down
as fast as it can.
It finds it
and tips
the earth
in a pile.

That's better!
But the man
in the cab
says,
'Hey! No rest for you!
There's more where that came from!'

At night
the driver
parks it
with its chin
on the ground,
looking at all
that earth.

I think
it's a sad life
for a digger.

Supermarket Robert

Robert loves trolleys.
He loves to steer.
He loves to cut the corners.
He loves to bump the wheels
Into other people's heels.

A Lesson

Darren took all
the labels off
the tins in Mummy's
shopping bag.

He sorted them
like teacher had,
red and yellow,
green and blue.

Tonight the dog
had soup for tea,
the cat had beans
and Darren had

Whiskas.
He said it
tasted horrible
on toast.

Uphill, Downhill

The day we went for a walk in the country,
Dad and Mum and my little brother and me
and the dog — ('Come here, Kipper! Now!') —
we walked uphill and downhill
and uphill and downhill again and
got lost.
Dad got out his map.
After twisting and turning it
he said, 'We must be here.'
So we walked uphill and downhill
and uphill and downhill and uphill again
and we were still lost.
My little brother Darren was crying.
He was afraid he'd never get home again.

Mum said,
'Give me that map!
No wonder we're lost!
You're holding it the wrong way up.'
Dad said,
'Have it your own way.
You always know best.'
So we walked uphill and downhill
and uphill and downhill and uphill again
and we were even more lost than before.

It was getting dark by now
and cold.

I said,
'I think it's this way, over there,'
and they said,
'Don't be daft.'

'But I recognize that tree.'

'Hark at her!' they said.
'How can you recognize trees?
You never looked at a tree in your life!'

The funny thing is
I was right.
The car was waiting for us
right behind the next wall.

The other funny thing is why,
when you go for a walk,
is there always more uphill than downhill?
Lots more.

Following the Smells

Down in the dark deep dirty depths of the ditch,
following the smells!

Rat smells, bird smells, fox smells!
How good my nose is!

How well it fits me, wet and snuffling!
Every day I sniff my thanks!

Lizard smell, toad smell, vole smell, worm smell!
Snuffle them up, good old nose!

Fox stood here
dead of night,

dreamed on paws
of filling belly,

stepped out of ditch,
through nettles pushed,

cross field, helter-skelter, helter-skelter —
slow, nose, slow! legs can't keep up! —

Crossed lane —
sniff, nose, sniff! —

Into ditch,
dark deep dirty depths of ditch!

Weasel smell, mouse smell, frog smell, beetle smell!
Chase, nose, chase!

The Farm Park

Six of them, with
one piggy mum.
A piggy litter.

Four piggy feet,
two piggy ears,
one piggy tail — each.

I fell in love with
the piglet that came up
for a fuss —

those legs
like stubby crayons
used too much —

its eyes like Kipper's,
sad and asking,
'Where's my next meal?'

Mum's on a Diet

Mum's on a diet.
She thinks she's fat.
She hardly eats anything.
She's still as
sleek as a cat.

I know why.
In the front room,
behind the books on the shelf,
she's hidden a box of chocolates.
When she's eaten one
she purrs.

Special Request

The day Mum had a record request on the radio
she was in the kitchen
putting the washing on.
We called her
and called her
and called her,
but all she said was,
'Turn that radio down!
I can't hear what you're saying.'
So we shouted again
as loud as we could
and in the end she came
just as the record was finishing.
'That's my favourite song,'
she said.
'Why didn't you call me?'
So we explained.
She's still not sure whether to believe us
or not.
'Me?' she said. 'Me?
A record for me?'

Dad's Bald

Dad's bald.
He's got
one hundred and fifty-two hairs
on the back of his head
like the rear half of a duchess's tiara.
I counted them once
during Cup Final
and tweaked a dozen more out
when he suddenly sat forward
and shouted, 'That ref needs glasses! *Ouch!*'
He's fat too
and waddles when he walks,
and his chins shake
when he laughs,
which is often.
People like him though.
I like him.
People stop him
when we're out.
'Hi! Jack!
Long time no see!'
'Who was that?' Mum says
when we've gone a decent distance.
'Don't you remember?
We met them
on that outing,' Dad says.
'I'm sure we didn't,' says Mum.
'But they certainly
remembered you!
What is it about you?'

Mum's thinner, quieter.
I look at them sometimes.
I wonder —
who shall I look like
when I grow up?

Short Back and Sides

We once had a lawnmower
would never do as it was told.

You just had to turn your back
and it would be giving the cat
a short-back-and-sides,
chewing the heads off the dahlias
or worrying the ends of the washing —

The shirts it ate! The trousers! The socks!
It loved the taste of socks!

Then one day it upped and left home,
plugged itself into the car battery
and raced off into the country.

'Let it go,' Dad said.
'Good luck to it. It's sad
that some lawnmowers just can't get used
to living in gardens.'

We saw it on the telly
a couple of days later.
It was mowing the countryside.
The Army had cornered it
with helicopters and machine-guns.
It disappeared into a field of corn
with a scarecrow riding on its back
and shouting, 'Attaboy!'

Dad switched the television off.
'From now on we'll do the lawn with scissors,'
was all he said.

Names

Things Dad calls Kipper

Nippy Noodle.
Pan Handler.
Pippa — his first owner
didn't know much about dogs.
Fish Face.
Worzel Gummidge.
In Your Basket!
You've just been out!
Goldilocks.
(Silly coot, Kipper thinks.
My colour's black and white!)
Yessir!
Germ raid!
Licker!

Things Kipper calls Dad

Baldilocks.
Spoilsport.
Short on the biscuits.

Last Day of Term

Daniel Lowndes and Richard Rowland,
sprawled on the carpet with their Segas.
Julie and David by the window
discussing their holiday in Antigua.

Teacher on a chair pulling staples and pins,
handing them down to Elysha Dunn —
'Your pictures will be on my table till half past
　three.'
— Last day of term. Another year gone.

'I'll miss you and miss you,' Jean Austin cries.
She clutches Miss's hand and hugs it to her chest.
'You're not going far,' Miss says, 'only fifty metres.
By October Mrs Hembrow will be the best

teacher you've ever had. Jean — let me go.
You know how busy I am this time of year.'
— Last day of term. How I love and hate you!
Empty desks and empty walls, my best friend
　Sarah

split from me into the other class because we talk.
New things to learn, old ways to forget.
You should *always* underline the date!
Whoever told you to join your s's like that?

Miss claps her hands. 'Final assembly now.
Wendy, line up! Don't dither girl!
Richard — that thing stays on your desk!' Then,
　almost sad,
'Thank you, class. It's been a lovely year.'

Home Time

(after Lorca)

The afternoon
turns cold.
The classroom windows steam up.

Suddenly
the children playing by the sink
cry out —
through the misted window
the tree at the edge of the playground
has caught fire.
It is growing yellow wings.
Look, teacher, look! It's flying!

Cold.
With a shiver
the afternoon lies down
on the far side of the playing fields.
It curls up
in a wisp of mist and night.

Pointing golden-apple cheek-red fingers
come from the sky
and tap on the roof-tops.
Quarter past three, they whisper.
Home time.
In the classroom
the teacher lines the children up.

Thank You

The cake on the table
with pink icing
left over from tea —

I said the dog took it
but I don't think
they believed me.

They said, 'Thank you
for putting the paper in the bin.
Thank you for washing up the plate.

'Thank you very much.
You were very thoughtful.
Oh, and did the cake taste nice?'

Bye, Cat

Cats.
Hate 'em.

All fur and fluff
and spit and eyes in the dark.

Hate them.
Grrr!

At least think I do.
Never caught one.

Always up trees,
or tops of walls,

or leering from windows,
milk on their whiskers,

slipping through hedges
and me on my lead —

always
out of reach.

Never caught one? Never?
A big dog like you? I don't believe a word of it!

OK, I tell a lie
(never told my best friend this).

Caught one once.
Surprised it in the garden.

Up I rushed,
all fangs and claws,

bark like a police siren
promising blue murder.

Didn't move, stupid thing.
Sat there blinking.

What can you do
when a cat won't fight back?

Lick her on the nose.
Bark, 'Got you, kitty.'

Retreat on tip-claw.
'Bye, cat. Bye, cat.'

Plenty of Time

The wind
ran along the street
collecting what it could carry,
leaves, dust, crisp bags, chocolate wrappers —
that sort of thing.

It meant to tidy things up
but it got bored.
It threw a plastic shopping bag
in the branches of a tree
and left it flapping there.

That'll keep them awake at nights,
it thought, *and make them think of me.*

Then it rattled off a dustbin lid
and bowled it down the garden path
past a startled cat
whose tail it tweaked.

It liked that. It did it again.
The cat spat and showed its sharp claws.
All right, the wind said.
I didn't mean any harm.
Honestly!

Then it saw a boy and girl.

Hey! it thought. *I'll pick them up.*
I'll pick them up and shove them on
the roof of that house, the red one,
They'd look funny up there!

So it came whistling at them.
Their hats flew off their heads.
Their scarves wrapped round them twice.
Their coats tugged at them to be off.
They put their heads down
but the wind came back at them,
trying to bowl them over
so it could pick them up.

Lucky we were so close to home, the boy said
when they got indoors.
I think that wind meant to carry us away.

What funny ideas you have! his mother said.
Whatever made you think that?

Outside the wind settled down to rest
in the tree by the front gate.
It twisted its fingers round the twigs.
Plenty of time, it thought.
All the time in the world.

The girl winked at it from the window.

Saturdays

Saturdays I visit Nan's.
Dad puts me on the bus
And pays my fare.
Nan meets me the other end.

First we wait for the milkman,
Then we go up the shops.
After, while she's cooking dinner,
I watch the video she's got.

Grandad died five years ago.
Framed photos of him
Are all around the house.
'I wish he'd seen baby Darren,'

Nan sometimes says. A sad look
Comes into her eyes.
'He was ever so fond of you.'
But I don't remember then.

At teatime Mum and Dad arrive
With Darren in his pram
And Kipper on his lead.
'Laura got it all,' says Gran.

Dad winks. He knows it's not true.
After we walk home in the dark.
Mum buys crisps
From the pub by the park.

Then it's time for bed.
That's my Saturday.

Small Talk

(after Lorca)

— Mother!
    I want to be silver.

— Treasure!
    you'd be very chill.

— Mother!
    let me be water.

— Treasure!
    the cold would make you ill.

— Mother!
    sew me in your cushion.

— Treasure!
    let me finish this stitch.

— Mother!
    I want to be good.

— Treasure!
    And so you should!

History

The bit of rag I carried
till I was three —
the scar on my thigh
when I fell from a tree.
      (You'll carry that for life,
        the doctor said.)

The programme from the panto
we saw when Grandad was still alive —
the watch he gave me
when I was five.
      (At the bottom of a drawer now.
        I broke it in a fight.)

A picture of Dad
in flares and winkle-picker shoes —
Kipper, as a puppy,
watching the News.
      (At least it looks as if he is —
        he's not that bright.)

The day Darren was born,
me both jealous and proud —
Darren five minutes ago,
bossy, disgusting, loud.
      (The sooner he turns
        into a human being the better!)

Gran at Mum and Dad's wedding
looking really young —
me in a party hat
sticking out my tongue.
      (*One day you'll be embarrassed by that!*
        Mum said. I already am!)

Somewhere in the middle of these
is the earliest thing I remember.
The latest? Well,
that's writing this.
      (Until I put the pencil down
        and move away, that is —)

Sledging

Gran remembers snow
ten feet deep on Kingscourt Lane,
the village school closed,
no buses,
no milk —

the power lines down,
no light and little heat
for four whole days,
the pile of coal in the coalhouse falling
lower and lower.

But mostly she remembers
sledging on Rodborough Common,
the hiss of the runners,
the world rushing up from the valley
and the bump at the bottom.

Windy Day

Sarah my friend jumps back in fright
as the wind gusts
and tries to tug her
from the pavement.

But me, I couldn't care less.
I love the wind
as it pulls me by the hair
and tries to turn me over.

I can out-run the wind
any time I want,
cartwheel faster,
somersault in half the time
from here to there.

Come on, wind!
Race me — if you dare!

Chocolate Santa

There was a chocolate Santa
on the Christmas tree at Gran's.
'Yours on Christmas Day,' she said,
'but not before. Good girls don't touch.'

He sparkled just above my nose
and smelt of silver paper and chocolate.
'Yours on Christmas Day,' she said.
'Remember — don't touch!'

I could taste him already.
How delicious he would be.
Every time I passed
my fingers itched.
'But not before Christmas day.
You're a good girl, aren't you?'

Two days before Christmas it was just too much.
I took him down and ate him, every bit —
beard, sack, greatcoat, the lot.
No chocolate ever tasted so awful,
No Santa ever tasted so bad.

'Good girls,' she said.
'Good girls don't touch.'

What, Me?

Bad-tempered? Me?
Throw my coat on the floor?
Say my dinner's yacky?
Storm out and slam the door?

You must be joking
Or thinking of someone else.
Or dreamed him in a nightmare.
You weren't thinking of yourself?

Now, did you say ice-cream for pudding?
My favourite.
A bargain.
Consider it done.

When you're old,
And I've grown up too,
I promise I'll be
Just as thoughtful as you.

When I was a Baby

When I was a baby
I couldn't walk.
I crawled
around the floor
making ga-ga noises.
I ate apples
and left the core
on the carpet.

Didn't know better.
Didn't know worse.

At breakfast
I bashed my egg on the head
so it spattered everywhere.
I put my socks
on my ears,
my trousers on my arms,
milk in the jam,
jam in the milk,
everything everywhere
except the right place.

Didn't know better.
Didn't know worse.

Mum says
I was a very good baby.
She wishes
I was good
like that now.

But I could be good like that any day! Honest!

Didn't know better.
Didn't know worse.
Now what do you make of that?

Trees

Long time ago
trees here.
Dozens.
Great-grandmother
told me.
Met her
in gutter
week ago
or two.
Not remember.
Not good
at figures.

Different then.
Many many trees.
Told me
so many
creature
would take
all summer
travel
one end
to other.

Said
tree there
where house stands
so tall
made
creature
dizzy.
Head in clouds.

On clear day
could see
sun rise
in other country.
All gone now.
Different now.
Silly old
great-grandmother.

Says dustbin
not good.
Still hankers
for acorns.
Says her
great-grandmother
remembered
the world
all trees.
No houses,
no shops,
no dual carriageways,
no playing
dare
with cars.
No dustbin.
Silly old
great-grandmother.

Fox

I saw it first —
Kipper needs glasses! —
a long shadow at dusk
that walked at running pace
across the gravelled lane
that climbs from the motorway,
up past the flats to our house.

The fox turned to look
as it stepped into the hedge.

Kipper whimpered and chased.
Within moments he was back.
His eyes avoided Dad's and mine.
His nose pointed homewards.

What words did the fox say
on the other side of the hedge
about being wild and free?
Only Kipper knows.

Old Man's Song

When I was young
my mother said,
'Keep out of the rain.
It addles your brain.'

So the first day it rained
I danced in the puddles,
and ran with the showers,
and rolled in the grass,
and lay down in the flowers.

The water ran out of
my ears and my toes,
it filled my pockets
and dripped from my nose.
The lightning flooded me,
the thunder showered me,
the storm clouds tickled
and patted and towelled me dry.

Back home my mother beat me
and put me to bed,
and, though I'm ninety-three,
the cold she gave me
has never gone away,
never gone away.

Weekends

All weekend
my Dad lies under the car,
all day, all night,
and Mum goes mad.

'There he goes banging about again,'
she says, 'the mess, the fiddle!'
clattering the dishes,
slamming the cooker door.

Dad shouts, 'Pass that spanner!
That hammer! That supaglue!
This car's falling to pieces!
Give me some patience!'

At five o'clock Monday he comes home
in a cloud of smoke.
He says, 'It's had it,
I ought to get rid of it.

'Didn't I? Didn't I?
I'll have my tea later.
Just make me a sandwich.'
But after it's, 'Jump in the car!

'Let's go for a spin.
It's a lovely evening, isn't it?
I love this car.'
Mum doesn't mind so much then.

Beach Howl

Sand, sand, everywhere,
Sand between my toes,
Sand in my costume,
Up my runny nose.

Sand in my bucket,
Sand in my pop,
Sand in my sandwiches,
In everything I've got.

Legs, legs, everywhere,
Knees and feet and shins,
Deck chairs, awnings,
Plastic rubbish bins.

Legs, legs, everywhere,
Red with sun and raw,
Joined to heads and bodies
I've never seen before.

Water, water, everywhere,
Right from right to left,
Water in the sea and in my eyes
Because suddenly I'm lost.

Send for the policeman!
Send for the cops!
They've left me in the lurch,
Dumped me on the rocks!

Out of the Sun

A kite,
red, white, blue,
shape of
a dragon —
Dad launched it.
With a flick
he sailed it
skywards.
It soared
tree-high,
house-high,
cloud-high.
Eye of a dragon
stared down at us.
Why didn't the clouds
swallow it?

'Want a go?'
Dad said,
crick-necked.
'What?' I gulped.
'No. Not me.'
Anyway he was enjoying himself.
I wandered off
along the hill.
Someone else
let me have a go at theirs.

Later he said,
'Did you see it?
Another dragon!
It swooped down on ours!
It tried to eat ours up!'

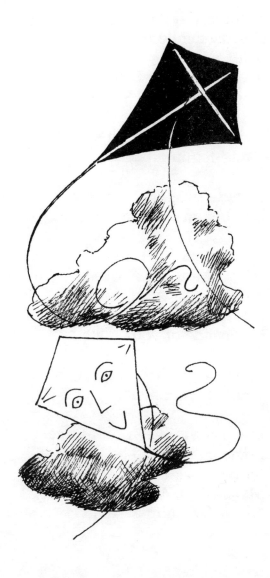

Manners

My mother told me
when I was a pup,

A crumb on the table's
best on the floor.

A crust on the carpet's
worth five on the plate.

A crisp in the mouth's
worth ten in a pack.

So here sit I,
best bib and tucker,

tail dusting the lino,
eyes shining with love.

Darren, darling — edge that chip
to the side of your plate.

Laura, sweetheart — everyone knows
you hate that meat.

Dad, my friend — don't forget:
rules are made to be broken.

Mum, Mum, Mum — don't say:
Never feed him at table.

Mum Says

Mum says, 'In the bathroom.
        Wash behind your ears.'
Dad says, 'Hurry, I'm desperate.
        You've been in there years.'

Dad says, 'Eat up now.
        We're late. Shovel it in.'
Mum says, 'Manners! Don't gobble!
        You've egg on your chin.'

Mum says, 'You need fresh air.
        Outside and play.'
Dad says, 'Off that lawn.
        Too wet for football today.'

Mum says, 'Turn the computer off.
        It's time to eat.'
Dad says, 'Only a second more!
        This game's really neat!'

Mum says, 'I want you in Bedfordshire.
        Now! It's getting late.'
Later she complains, 'You let me fall asleep.'
        'You snore,' I say. 'You keep me awake.'

After the Party

After the party,
the disco dancing,
the pass-the-parcel,
the noise and shouting,
I ran upstairs.

In my room
I found moonlight
laid across the bed.

In a twinkle of the eye,
the second it took to close the curtains,
it rolled itself up
and slipped outside.

It lay across the garden
as quietly as before.

Get You

He drew a monster
on the inside cover
of his library book.
That was at bedtime,
but he fell asleep.

By morning
the monster
seemed bigger,
its eyes
more open wide,
its ears more pointed.
A drop of blood
flecked its chin.

By bedtime
that night
it was inching towards
the edge of the paper.
As he quickly closed the book
the monster grinned.

Snow

By nine
the storm's blown out.
A thousand stars
blossom in the sky.

The cars huddle
like beached whales
in the street.
Beneath the bedroom window
a red fox
pads across the lawn.

In Moonlight

(after Lorca)

The moon treads across the water.
The water laps to and fro.
How long has this been going on?
Only moon and water know.

On the far side of the river
A young branch combs its leaves.
To and fro lap the waters.
The bank shivers in the breeze.

'Moon? What nonsense! The very idea!'
The trees' voices grow shrill.
'This is our silver mirror —
like us restless — never still.'

Moon treads across water.
Water laps to and fro.
How long has this been going on?
Only the moon and water know.

I Love it Late at Night

I love it late at night —
half a dozen cars,
the yellow street lights
stretching away
into the distance.

Night silence —
the journey home
from relatives
or a special treat,
or the time we went ten-pin bowling.

Between trees and roof-tops
the moon weaves in and out.
Cats' eyes flash
from wall tops.
A gate swings to and fro.

Milk bottles in rows
stand waiting for dawn —
a downstairs room
full of TV light —
a bedroom window goes suddenly dark.

Turning, by the park,
two fox cubs
gambol on the verge.
Dazzled, front paws frozen,
they snarl and fall apart.

The car draws up.
A shadow from the flower-beds
wraps around your ankles.
Key in the lock.
Welcome, the house says, where have you been?

Lost in a Forest

I'm lost in a forest,
all alone,
no family, no friends,
no bed, no home.

I run through the trees
but the snow clogs my feet.
A bear in a cave
wants something to eat.

A pack of wolves
howls in full cry.
I stumble and fall.
I don't want to die.

I'm lost in a forest,
all alone,
when a voice says,
'Wake up. It's only a dream.

'What was it? A snake?
A monster? A ghost?'
'Nothing,' I cry.
I sob in Mum's arms.

Candle

The night of the power cut,
when everything went off,
they put a candle in my room.
I went to sleep by candle light.

Every time I woke
the candle's soft light
was flickering
on the chest of drawers.

It lit my dreams.

Sleep

The thing I hate most in the world
is going to bed.
All the best telly's on
after bedtime,
isn't it?
Sleep! How can you sleep
with all the rest of the world
alive and awake?
Downstairs I can hear
Mum and Dad talking,
outside older children
playing in the street.
Darren starts crying
and Dad takes him down.
It's not fair! It's not fair!
Why him?
Why not me down there?

Then it gets dark.
The street goes quiet.
The odd car.
A gate clanging.
A dog barks.
Someone hushes it.
I can't see my hand
in front of my face any more.
Night fills
every corner of the room.
Mum brings Darren back up.
They've shut the backroom door.
At last I can feel
sleep coming,

a long way off at first,
but coming closer.
Closer and closer it comes.
It's almost here, almost . . .

Lullaby

(after Lorca)

The evening's slow fingers
were singing
the orange groves
to sleep.
You want to know how?

Ninna nanna, ninna nanna,
the lullaby went.

And my brother was singing
at the top of his voice —
the world is an orange,
the world is an orange.

Ninna nanna, ninna nanna,
the lullaby went.

That set the moon off.
I want to be an orange!
I want to be an orange too!
The tears ran down its face.

I laughed at the moon.
I said — impossible, silly.
Even if you said your prayers
till your cheese turned pink,
not even a lemon
we'd squeeze out of you!
What a shame!

Ninna nanna, ninna nanna,
the lullaby went.

Kipper

I have four people,
Mum and Laura,
Darren and Dad.
When it's dark
I lie in the hall,
Tail flat on the floor,
Tongue ready to bark.

Night-Time

Like a fox
darkness creeps in
through the trees.
There's a fire
in the sky.
Suddenly
the hills
disappear.
The stars
put out the fire.
In the fields
the little ghosts
shiver.

Index of Titles

A Lesson 25
After The Party 64

Beach Howl 59
Bye, Cat 40

Candle 71
Carthorses 12
Chocolate Santa 50

Dad's Bald 32
Dawn 9

Earth Eater 22

First Day 14
Following the Smells 28
Fox 56

Get You 65
Good Morning 10

History 46
Home Time 38

I Love it Late at Night 68
In Moonlight 67

Keep Your Feet Dry 16
Kipper 76

Last Day of Term 36
Lost in a Forest 70
Lullaby 74

Manners 62

Mum Says 63
Mum's on a Diet 30

Names 35
Night-Time 77

Old Man's Song 57
Out of the Sun 60

Pigeons 13
Pin Drop 15
Plenty of Time 42

Saturdays 44
Short Back and Sides 34
Sledging 48
Sleep 72
Small Talk 45
Snow 66
Special Request 31
Supermarket Robert 24

Thank You 39
The Crane 20
The Farm Park 29
The Dragon in the Playground 18
Trees 54

Uphill, Downhill 26

Weekends 58
What, Me 51
When I was a Baby 52
Windy Day 49
Wrong 19

Yawn 11

Index of First Lines

A kite 60
After the party 64
All weekend 58

Bad-tempered? Me? 51
By nine 66

Cats 40

Dad's bald 32
Daniel Lowndes and Richard
  Rowland 36
Darren took all 25
Down in the dark deep dirty
  depths of the ditch 28

Good morning! 10
Gran remembers snow 48

He drew a monster 65
How slow can a clock tick? 18

I have four people 76
I love it late at night 68
I saw it first 56
I'm lost in a forest 70
It was so noisy before school 15
Its long neck reaches out high over
  the houses 20

Kevin Cooper tricked me 19

Like a fox 77
Long time ago 54

Mist rolls past 9
– Mother! 45
Mum says, 'In the bathroom' 63

Mum's on a diet 30
My mother told me 62

Red cave 11
Robert loves trolleys 24

Sand, sand everywhere 59
Sarah my friend jumps back in
  fright 49
Saturdays I visit Nan's 44
Six of them, with 29

The afternoon 38
The bit of rag I carried 46
The cake on the table 39
The day Mum had a record request
  on the radio 31
The day we went for a walk in the
  country 26
The digger 22
The evening's slow fingers 74
The man with the pigeons 13
The moon treads across the water
  67
The night of the power cut 71
The street growled 14
The thing I hate most in the
  world 72
The wind 42
There was a chocolate Santa 50
They lie side by side 12
Things Dad calls Kipper 35

We once had a lawnmower 34
When I was a baby 52
When I was young 57
'Wear your hat,' Mum said 16